30 Minutes
... To Manage
Your Time Better

Tony Atherton

KOGAN
PAGE

First published 1999

Apart from any fair dealing for the purposes of research or private study, or criticism or review, as permitted under the Copyright, Designs and Patents Act 1988, this publication may only be reproduced, stored or transmitted, in any form or by any means, with the prior permission in writing of the publishers, or in the case of reprographic reproduction in accordance with the terms and licences issued by the CLA. Enquiries concerning reproduction outside these terms should be sent to the publishers at the undermentioned address:

Kogan Page Limited
120 Pentonville Road
London N1 9JN

British Library Cataloguing in Publication Data
A CIP record for this book is available from the British Library.

ISBN 0 7494 3056 7

Typeset by JS Typesetting, Wellingborough, Northants
Printed and bound by Clays Ltd, St Ives plc

CONTENTS

The 30 Minutes Series

The *Kogan Page 30 Minutes Series* has been devised to give your confidence a boost when faced with tackling a new skill or challenge for the first time.

So the next time you're thrown in at the deep end and want to bring your skills up to scratch or pep up your career prospects, turn to the *30 Minutes Series* for help!

Titles available are:

30 Minutes Before a Meeting
30 Minutes Before a Presentation
30 Minutes Before Your Job Appraisal
30 Minutes Before Your Job Interview
30 Minutes To Boost Your Communication skills
30 Minutes To Brainstorm Great Ideas
30 Minutes To Deal with Difficult People
30 Minutes To Get Your Own Way
30 Minutes To Make the Right Decision
30 Minutes To Make the Right Impression
30 Minutes To Market Yourself
30 Minutes To Master the Internet
30 Minutes To Motivate Your Staff
30 Minutes To Plan a Project
30 Minutes To Prepare a Job Application
30 Minutes To Succeed in Business Writing
30 Minutes To Write a Business Plan
30 Minutes To Write a Marketing Plan
30 Minutes To Write a Report

Available from all good booksellers.
For further information on the series, please contact:

Kogan Page, 120 Pentonville Road, London N1 9JN
Tel: 0171 278 0433 Fax: 0171 837 6348

BEING EFFECTIVE

Life is too short to let even one day
be frenzied or frazzled or frittered away.
Life is too short not to take time to do the things that
will hold the most meaning for you.

Verse on a Hallmark Greetings Card

Time – the eternal problem! As a child, you have time to
fill and 'nothing to do', and as an adult, you have too much
to do and too little time to do it in.

Is time management the panacea to this adult problem,
or is it just a myth about lists, lists and more lists? Time
management is not about clock-watching, nor is it about
timing everything to the nearest minute – even 30 minutes.
In a sense it is not even about managing time – it is about
managing yourself.

Time management may demand a change in your attitude towards your life and work and the things you want
to do. In return, it will help you to regain control over your

work and life by recognizing what is really important and what is not, and by doing the important things instead of the unimportant ones.

To use the principles of time management you need to know what the really important things are in your life and at work and give them a high priority – and that includes your home and family. Of course, other things will intrude, but your task is to recognize the intruders you do not want and control them so that they do not take over. If you can answer the following questions then you are on your way to being a good time manager.

What are the most important things you want to do:

- today;
- this week;
- this month?

There are a few core time management skills to learn and master. They are easy to use but it takes perseverance to keep on using them, day in and day out, and turn them into habits. You may need to crush old habits and build these fresh skills into a new and permanent way of working. Only then will you reap the benefits in full.

As well as the core skills many other suggestions are given in this book. Some will be important to you and some not. Choose according to what suits you and your work.

Gradually building new habits is the key to success, but there are three cheering lessons to learn right now:

- *You are not alone.* Surveys repeatedly show that employees are working longer and longer and want to break from this habit.

- *You cannot do everything*. If you do the important things 'they' will not worry too much about the unimportant ones, and neither should you.

- *Feeling more in control reduces stress*. These habits will put you back in control.

How much more effective will you be? To estimate how well you manage your time now, try the quiz below. Then, after using the principles outlined in this book for about a month, do the quiz again. It does not matter much what you score the first time around but you should find that your score increases by 10 to 20 points after a month. The average increase is about 15. However approximate the measure, it is a very significant result.

Time Management Quiz

Rate yourself, from 0 (poor) to 5 (excellent):

1 I am absolutely clear about what is important to me.
2 I have clear goals at work, in line with my performance objectives.
3 I prioritize all my work goals.
4 I feel in control of events at work.
5 I use a few minutes to plan each week and day.
6 I stick to the important tasks throughout the working day.
7 I recognize tasks that are not really important, even when they are urgent.
8 I force myself to make time for the important things.
9 I often say 'no' to tasks that are not really important, or not really my job.

10 I recognize trivia, and deal with it quickly and effectively.

11 I control interruptions, including telephone calls, really well.

12 My work area/office is well organized, I find things when I want them.

13 There is harmony between my private life and ambitions and my work.

14 I do not forget commitments I have made, and I complete them.

15 When I commit time to something, I know it will be available.

16 My diary/organizer, whether paper or electronic, is indispensable to me.

17 I get home at a sensible time and only take work home if I choose to.

18 I keep my stress to a manageable level.

19 I have quite precise definitions of key things I want to achieve.

20 I prioritize the day's tasks every day.

Total (out of 100): Now: After one month:

Improving your personal effectiveness by using time management techniques is not difficult but it does need tenacity. Some people have likened it to losing weight: you know what to do – make a permanent change to your diet – but will you do it? It is the same with time management. This book will tell you what to do. Your challenge is to make the permanent changes to the way you work, little by little, over the next few weeks. Be firm with yourself and build these new habits, starting now.

To choose time is to save time. (Francis Bacon)

2

WHERE DOES YOUR TIME GO?

There are 168 hours in every week but some weeks it feels as if we have been short-changed. Where did the time go? What have I done today? These are familiar questions to millions of people.

The answers revolve around five things you can do. We will look at how to do them in the rest of the book. The five things are:

1 Develop your awareness of the importance of your time and how you use it.

2 Know what the really important things are that you want to do, in your private life and at work.

3 Give those things a high priority and mean it.

4 Ensure that your priorities get the time they need, while being pleasant and helpful to others and playing your full role in the team.

5   Recognize what and who steal your time and deal with
    them pleasantly but effectively.

Diaries and organizers are important, vital for many people,
but not as important as your attitude to making good
use of your time. Without an attitude of caring about, and
being aware of your use of time, no diary will solve your
problems.

Raising your awareness of time

The first step to developing awareness of the importance
of your time is to know where time goes. Knowing this is
also the first step to controlling it better. Despite the saying
'time is money', time is not money. You can usually earn
more money and spend less if you really want to. With
time, you cannot earn more and you cannot use less. It
comes – and goes – at the same old rate, whatever you do.

Try thinking about a 24-hour day as having four classes
of time (see Figure 2.1). Some activities could naturally fall
under more than one classification. That does not matter.
For many people it is the competition between work time
and the others that is the problem that has to be solved.

Classifications of the 24-hour day

- *Health time:* the time you need to keep yourself healthy
  – sleeping, eating, resting, exercising, spiritual time.
- *Work time:* the time you sell or give to other people –
  your employment, charity work, scouts, guides and so
  on.
- *Family time:* the time you devote to your family and
  home.

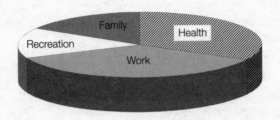

Figure 2.1 *Classifications of time: the 24-hour day*

- *Recreation time:* the time you use as you wish, by yourself or with others, for recreation, relaxation – sports, television, reading, etc.

Many people feel pressured into spending more time at work, sometimes to the insane level of competing with one another to see who can stay the longest. Quite simply, more time at work means less time for health, family and recreation.

This problem often starts with creeping assaults on your recreation and family times. They shrink. You get home later or leave earlier in the morning. Is this wrong? That is up to you. Do you really want to spend less time with your family and friends and more time at work? Or is now the time to ask yourself: 'What do I really want to do?'

As work takes up ever more hours, eventually your health time is attacked. You skip lunch or eat a sandwich at your desk. You skip breaks. You lose sleep. Your work suffers and eventually your health suffers. Now it is serious. Continue like this and you could be on the way to a heart attack, a mental breakdown or a divorce – or even all three. It happens to real people like you.

> Has there ever been a deathbed 'confession that said: 'I should have spent more time at work?'

Of course, work pressures are real. You have to earn a living. You have bills to pay and a mortgage. Less pressured jobs are not easy to find.

To regain control you must decide, given your circumstances, to be more aware of how much time should be devoted to your health, family, work and recreation. Consider this carefully. Do you work a lot of unpaid overtime every week? What has happened to your life? What are your real priorities?

> Surveys suggest that some managers work at least 15 hours a week more than their contract requires. That is equivalent to an extra two days a week. What would your boss say if you gave a customer an extra 40 per cent free – every week?

Now decisions: the Maltese Cross dilemma

Time management is about improving effectiveness by doing the right things – the important things – at the right time and at the expense of the unimportant. It is not normally about improving efficiency. That can be a later, separate task. There is little point in being super-efficient if you are doing the wrong things in the first place.

Every day we make innumerable decisions about what to do next, that is, what to do 'now'. Success hinges on our ability to put the important things first on most of those

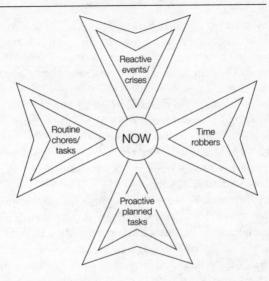

Figure 2.2 *The Maltese Cross dilemma: the demands on your time*

dozens or hundreds of occasions every day when we decide 'what to do now'. We can plan for the future, we can reminisce about the past, but we make decisions now.

At work, four broad types of events compete for your attention at that moment called 'now'. These are represented as a Maltese Cross in Figure 2.2. Control these when deciding what to do 'now' and you will not need to do an extra 15 hours of unpaid overtime every week.

Proactive planned tasks are the important things you plan to do. They should stem from your work and personal goals, or objectives, or whatever you want to call them. These tasks move you or the company forward.

9

Routine chores and tasks that will only take a few minutes and now might be a good time to do them. Doing them will never move you forward but ignoring them will hold you back. They are chores, like filing, and they can gobble up time if you are not careful.

Reactive events, mini-crises happen all around you every day. You could lend a hand right now. They are not your responsibility but you like to help.

Time robbers ambush you. Someone tells you about his or her holiday, or you need to ask someone, again, to show you how to do a tricky job.

Why is there never enough time for the important planned events? You know why – it is because you spend too much time on the other three arms of the Maltese Cross.

Every hour spent doing the chores, or showing you are very helpful, or listening to gossip is an hour less for the important things. Of course there must be some time for these other things. Chores must be done. You need to be co-operative. Working without social interaction would be unbearable. Do these things but raise your awareness of the importance of your time and learn to control the time given to less important things. Or continue working an extra 15 hours of unpaid overtime every week. The choice is yours.

Remember, it is achieving your goals – the important things that really matter – that determines your achievements, career progress and how much time you spend at work, not chit-chat and chores. Even when achieving your goals you should devote time to the most important ones. You may have to compromise lesser goals to make time for the major ones.

> Spending too much time on less important things
> =
> Working late to catch up on more important ones.

Time log

So where does your time go? Estimate or measure it against
the four arms of the Maltese Cross. It is not exciting but
the rewards are worth the effort. Try logging your time for
a period. The results could surprise you and at least you
will have accurate information on which to base some
decisions.

Tips

- Overcome differences between days and weeks by
  logging your time for Monday of one week, Tuesday
  of the next, and so on.

- Use classifications that are important to you, maybe the
  four arms of the Maltese Cross, or the four segments
  of the 24-hour cycle in Figure 2.1, or interruptions/
  telephone calls/meetings/tasks, etc.

- Do not estimate times at the end of the day, you will be
  more accurate if you make notes every half-hour or
  hour through the day.

You may be surprised, even shocked, at what you discover.
Once you have your facts, you can examine them critically
and decide what you need to change. This book will give
you plenty of ideas about how to change, but only you
can decide what to change.

Reactive or proactive

Every job demands that we react to events around us (the events and crises in the Maltese Cross) but employers expect us to shape events as well, to be proactive. Only one arm of the Maltese Cross is devoted to proactive tasks. To be more proactive and less reactive you need to spend more time on the planned activities and less on reacting to events, time robbers, routine tasks and chores. Be more proactive in how you use your time.

How proactive are you now? On the scale shown in Figure 2.3, mark where you feel you are at present between being totally proactive and totally reactive. Then mark where you would like to be. It is nearly always more to the right. That is your target. Make the shift in the next month, two at the most.

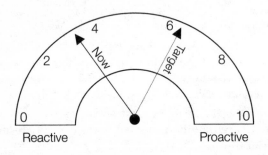

Figure 2.3 *Proactive versus reactive*

3

THINGS IMPORTANT
TO YOU

For many people the demands of work thwart private
ambitions. You have wanted to climb a mountain in Africa,
or do a long-distance walk, but you have not had the time.
Important jobs at work are rushed because there is no time.
The truth is that you have had the time, 168 hours a week
just like everyone else. You have simply given higher priority to other things.

If other things take over from private ambitions or work
objectives then a planning technique that puts important
things in their rightful place will be useful. Either that or
forget them.

Of the four arms of the Maltese Cross (Figure 2.2, page
9) the one that brings the richest rewards is that for proactive planned tasks. Good planning followed by good
action should enable you to do more of the things that are
important to you.

In reality however, your success depends on how you decide what you will do 'now'. Most people are easily blown by the wind of events into doing whatever seems to be expected of them by others or by what seems urgent, even if not particularly important. They may have a 'to do' list or use yesterday's list, but it gets scant attention after the first few moments because it is events that dictate their day. At the end of the day they are left wondering, 'What have I achieved today?'

It is trite, but planning begins by deciding what is important. When John F Kennedy announced that the United States was going to put a man on the moon and bring him back safely to earth by the end of 1969, he laid a goal before the US people and US industry. That goal had two important aspects: it specified what was to be done and it specified when it had to be completed. You need both of these, the what and the when, in your own planning.

Planning is a straightforward process, but it needs to become a habit:

- Decide what is important to you, your goals.

- Prioritize these goals and set sensible deadlines.

- Break down each goal into subordinate tasks, with deadlines.

- Schedule those tasks to specific months.

- Write a new 'to do' list every day or week, including:

    - proactive items from the month's tasks (from your important goals);

    - other tasks or chores that must be done.

14

- Start each day with two or three minutes' planning time.
- Schedule your week and day, allowing spare time to react to some unexpected events and crises.

Goals and tasks

Goals are those important things you want to achieve, whether at work or in your private life. They are the things that move you and the company forward rather than simply prevent you from slipping back. They are almost certainly too big for you to just go out and do them there and then. They will need to be broken down into their parts (the tasks) and you need to decide when you are going to do those tasks – the week or month will probably do at this stage.

Example: **Suppose you want to make a will**

It is unlikely that you could simply sit down and write a will that would meet any legal problems that might arise. You may decide to use a solicitor and for that you will need an appointment. You may also want to discuss your will with your spouse, maybe with other people as well. Perhaps you want to consider various people's feelings and sentiments towards some of your possessions. All of these tasks take time and thought. So it is with all goals.

Many people find private goals harder to achieve than work goals. At work, if you make no progress, someone is likely to push you by asking awkward questions. In your

15

private life you have to push yourself. A good planning method will serve to pressure you into achieving your private goals.

Don't like goals

Quite a lot of people do not like the concept of goals. They see them as being overly organized or restricting spontaneity. While that can be true it is usually a misconception. If you do not like 'goals' call them something else. A goal is simply one of those things that you really want to do. In the words of the poem at the beginning of Chapter 1, they are 'the things that will hold the most meaning for you'. But give them a deadline or they may never happen.

Your goals

What were you doing five years ago? What job did you have? Who were your friends? What was work like then? What was life like then? Does it really seem like five years have passed? What have you achieved since then?

Five years from now, what will you have achieved? That is where your goals come in.

Think ahead using the four questions which follow. Brainstorm the answers. Write them down in four groups without (at the moment) judging how practical you think they are. Judge that later.

1 *In your private life:* what are the really important things you want to achieve in the next few years?

2 *In your career:* what are the really important things you want to achieve in the next few years?

3 *In your private life:* what are the really important things you want to achieve in the next few months?

4 *At work:* what are the really important things you want to achieve in the next few months?

Now bring judgement into play. Do you really mean these things? Will you commit the time to achieve them? If there are any that you are not committed to, cross them off now. Then combine the lists and decide the priorities. Select your top priorities and keep this list somewhere safe, preferably in your diary or organizer.

Key Habit: Know what you want to do — your goals — and plan how and when to do them.

Split your goals into tasks

Treat your most important goal as you would a work project. (Later, do this for your other goals.)

- Define the goal more specifically if that will help.

- Decide when you want it to be completed. Be precise.

- Break down each goal into the tasks or steps that are needed to complete it.

- Arrange the tasks in the sequence in which they will have to be done.

- Give each task a deadline, just the month might do for now.

Example: **Cycle to Spain**

Goal:
For the fun of it, to cycle from the north coast of France to Spain and return by ferry, next October (assume it is now April).

Tasks:
- Telephone doctor to arrange a medical: Tomorrow
- Plan a fitness programme, visit gym to seek advice: Saturday
- Buy good maps of France and Northern Spain: Saturday
- Get ferry timetables from travel agent: Saturday
- Start cycling fitness programme: Sunday
  Targets:
  May: 15 miles per ride
  June: 25 miles per ride
  July: 35 miles per ride
  August: 50 miles per ride
  September: 70 miles per ride
- Learn cycle maintenance from a friend: May
- Calculate time needed, including rest days; book leave, book ferries: May
- Start gym fitness programme: end May
- Plan route; get details of small hotels in France and Spain: June
- Decide on kit needed; buy kit: June
- Have bike checked out; buy spares: September
- GO!   October

Example: **Improve swimming and fitness, and spend more time with my children**

Aim:

To swim 24 continuous lengths by this time next year.

Plan:

Swim each week, Tuesday evenings, and take children with me as a family outing. Get them to encourage and challenge me. (Buy them a treat at the end of each month – if I meet my target.)

Tomorrow: Telephone leisure centre to ask about swimming classes. Book as appropriate.

Month 1: complete two continuous lengths.

Month 2: complete four continuous lengths.

Month 3: complete six continuous lengths, etc.

Month 12: complete 24 continuous lengths.

Deciding priorities

Deciding priorities is one of the key habits to build. Too often we simply assume that everything has the same priority, but that is not the case. People say, 'Everything is important.' That may be true – but they are not of equal importance.

Also, we easily give too much time to things simply because they are urgent, or because someone shouts loudly, not because they are important. So often, urgent matters, that in the great scheme of things are not particularly important, take over from things that really matter but can wait until tomorrow, except that tomorrow may never come.

Juggling urgent and important

It is vital to recognize that there are scales of importance and urgency. Some tasks are important and some are not. Some tasks are urgent and some are not. The sense of urgency, with its demands for immediate action, distorts the impression of importance and leads us to give too much time to things simply because they are urgent. For example, if you are running out of petrol then it is urgent that you fill up, but it is not important which filling station you use. Driving an extra 10 miles to get loyalty points is foolish and wastes time, especially if you run out of petrol *en route*.

> The fact that something is urgent tells you nothing about its importance. Keep the two concepts separate.

When judging priorities consider both importance and urgency:

- *Important and urgent:* it must be done and you will benefit from its completion. Do it now and give it the time it deserves.

- *Urgent but low importance:* is it important to someone else? Does that change your view? Is it really someone else's problem? Do it soon but spend as little time on it as possible. Should you delegate it if you can?

- *Important but not urgent:* ideal! This is what your life and work is really for. Plan when to do it and give it as much unhurried time as appropriate.

- *Low importance and not urgent:* does it really have to be done? Who says so? Why spend time on it that could be better spent on something that is important? If there is no satisfactory answer, do not do it. If you still feel it ought to be done, delay it until one of those days when nothing seems to go right.

In the box which follows, there are some examples of the differences.

Important and urgent

- An unexpected visit from a major customer.
- Sorting out a production problem.
- Your child has been taken sick at school and you are needed.

Urgent but low importance

- An unexpected visit from a sales person from a minor supplier.
- A member of your staff is asking for leave tomorrow.
- A routine meeting.

Important but not urgent

- Preventing production problems in the future.
- Your child wants you to teach her to play chess.
- Your business or budget plan for next year.

Low importance and not urgent

■ Striving for the final bit of perfection in a report you have written.

■ Idle chit-chat and gossip.

■ Improving a spreadsheet that works well enough.

The 80:20 rule

It is generally true that your most important achievements do not take up most of your time. The 80:20 rule suggests that something like 20 per cent of what you do produces around 80 per cent of your really important results. If you can identify the things that are really important and give them more time then you can hope to achieve more. The rule applies to all sorts of activities:

■ 80 per cent of sales come from 20 per cent of your customers;

■ 80 per cent of your fun is from time spent with 20 per cent of your friends;

■ 80 per cent of your problems come from 20 per cent of your staff, or customers, or machines.

In reality, the ratio may be 70:30 or 60:40 for you, but think how this generic rule applies in your life and work. Use it to help you to determine your priorities better:

■ Which 20 per cent of your sites, machines, staff, customers or suppliers give you 80 per cent of your problems? Would extra time spent attending to them now pay dividends for the future?

- Which 20 per cent of your tasks achieve 80 per cent of your results?
- Which 20 per cent of your time at home builds your family life the most?

ABC priorities

It is helpful to have a method of assigning priorities. A simple but very effective and very widely used method is to prioritize tasks according to three levels. These three levels might be things that you must do, should do, or could do. Often they are simply called A, B and C.

Key Habit: Prioritizing

A = must do, highest priority, those things of greatest importance to you.

B = should do, medium priority.

C = could do, low priority, the nice to do's.

Think about your A priority tasks. These will come from your proactive planned goals, from routine tasks or chores and from reacting to events around you. Decide which is the most important of all and call this your A1 task. The next most important is your A2, and so on. Do not fool yourself with any nonsense about them all being A1s. These are all As, they are all important but they are not all A1s. They never have been and never will be.

The B and C tasks can simply be left as Bs and Cs. Numbering them is a waste of time. You will rarely have time to finish all your As let alone worry about the Bs. If you do, then you can reprioritize them as As.

To Do lists

To Do lists have been called all the names under the sun, from 'the most common factor between successful people' to 'shopping lists that never get used'. Used well and intelligently, they are the simplest and greatest help to gaining control and doing the important things.

Despite the mythology that has been built up around them, To Do lists are simple things. Instead of trying to remember everything you want to do today or this week, simply write them all down, prioritize them and tick things off as you complete them. That is a To Do list.

Although they strike some people as a novelty, it is a fair bet that the first To Do lists were written in cuneiform by Sumerians about 5,000 years ago, soon after writing was invented. If an archaeologist ever digs one up, I would expect to see that the C tasks had not been completed!

The written To Do list is the key to turning planning into achieving. Depending on the nature of your job you should use either a daily list or a weekly one but I prefer a daily one, if possible.

Many people use a To Do list but do not get the best advantage from it. Some hold their list in their head, often forgetting items on it, while others keep a written list to which they add new items every day so that the list grows and grows. To use a To Do list well:

■ Make a new list at the start of every day or week.

■ Include one or more tasks from your personal goals on every list.

■ Write the list in the same place each time, ideally in your diary.

- Rigorously prioritize it into As, Bs and Cs.
- Use it to drive what you do.
- Start with the most important item, A1, then the A2 and so on.
- Do not expect to complete everything on it.
- Tick off ✓ items as they are completed, or cross them off ✗ or carry them forward (c/f) to a future list – tomorrow or next week.
- Account for every item on your previous list: ticked, crossed, or carried forward. Unaccounted items may get forgotten.

Key Habit: Use a new, written and prioritized To Do list each day or week. Use it to drive what you do.

Reactive tasks

If something new arises during the day, as it surely will, add it to your To Do list and judge its priority honestly against the other items already there. Do not make it the A1 simply because it is new or exciting or because someone says it is urgent. If it genuinely is the new A1, treat it as such. If it is not, prioritize it accordingly.

Table 3.1 *Example of a To Do list*

Priority	Task	Action
A3	Telephone Neil – contract	✓
C	Phone Jenny – fees	✗
B	See Helen – new staff	c/f
A4	Finalize ABC report	✓
A2	Submit monthly budget	✓
A1	Call travel agent – holiday	✓
A5	Get Helen a new bike pump	c/f
C	Clear store cupboard	c/f
B	See Alan – his training	c/f

One manager, tired of keeping his To Do lists on bits of paper, decided to type them into his word processor. Daily the list grew as new items were added faster than old ones were deleted. When the list had grown to five close-typed A4 pages he decided there must be a better way. Each day had added a further indictment to the fact that he was failing to do the things he wanted to do.

4

SCHEDULING

How much you need to schedule your time will depend on the type of work you do and only you can decide. If you have many appointments and meetings, which differ from day to day, then you will need to schedule carefully. If your days follow a fairly fixed routine then your need to schedule carefully will be lower. Whatever level of detail you need, one thing is certain: there is no point in planning a schedule for every minute of the day. Keep your schedule flexible as you will always need some time for the unexpected.

Try to achieve a balance between your To Do list and your schedule. For example, there is no point in having a long To Do list if the day is filled end-to-end with meetings. If most of your time is committed to appointments and meetings then it is probably better to think of your To Do list as being for tomorrow, not today. Anything you do today will be a bonus.

Tip

When writing items in your schedule, block them off from the start time to the expected finish time. Try to avoid accepting commitments to meetings that are open-ended. Always ask for the finish time.

Do the As

After writing your To Do list always start the day with your A1, as you have just decided that it is your highest priority. We nearly all have a tendency to start with a C because, 'It will only take a moment'. Often those moments turn into half-hours. If you think about it, starting with the trivia really is a ridiculous way to work. It is perfectly normal not to have time to do the Bs and Cs. If they ever become As, they will get done.

Key Habit: Start with the A1.

Prime time

Busy schedules make it difficult to find time even for the As. A-tasks usually need lengthy periods of concentration if they are to be achieved well. Your A1 may need a couple of hours of effort, maybe a lot more. Giving it five minutes here and five minutes there is not an effective way of tackling it. It needs a concentrated period, yet most days at work can be consumed by interruptions, telephone calls, people dropping in, the in-tray, appointments, meetings and so on.

28

Meetings, appointments, reactive tasks or anything from the three reactive arms of the Maltese Cross can fill your schedule and make it impossible to give time to the proactive tasks that move you forward. It is vital, therefore, that you reserve time for these A-tasks. People have different names for this time: prime time, A time, red time. Whatever you call it, it is essential that you have it and protect it.

Schedule this prime time into your diary. Then if anyone rings to check if you are free you have a block in your diary that will force you to stop and think. Which is more important, that you spend time on your A1 or that you give this time to the caller? As we seem to regard meetings as a protected species try to regard your prime time as a meeting with your A1. Schedule it as you would any other important meeting and give it the protection it deserves. A simple slash across an hour or two in your schedule will work wonders for your productivity.

Key Habit: Schedule prime time into your diary as a meeting with your A1.

If a certain time of day is when you perform best then make it prime time whenever you can.

C tasks

You will always have lots of C-tasks, life is full of them, unimportant things that masquerade as important and clutter up your time. Do not be fooled. Life is too important to do Cs. However, Cs are sneaky things, changing into As when your back is turned.

Apply the 80:20 rule:

- 20 per cent of C-tasks will have to be done, now or later. They will become problems if ignored. Plan when to do them.

- 80 per cent of C-tasks do not have to be done. Forget them.

- Identify repetitive C-tasks and eliminate them from your work.

- A bank eliminated two repetitive C-tasks. They stopped returning cheques when customers made small mistakes:
    1) The words and numbers did not quite match; and
    2) Early in the New Year when customers wrote the previous year's date.
- A retail chain eliminated C-grade management forms.
- A service company eliminated monthly statistical analyses for small customers when it found that they did not understand them. It sent short written reports instead.
- A new manager changed from monthly to quarterly reports once his senior managers trusted his judgement.

Routine chores and tasks

One arm of the Maltese Cross was dedicated to routine chores and tasks, things which will not move you forward but will hold you back if ignored. Decide if they must be done at all and which are genuinely yours. Would it be fair to ask someone else to do them? Either plan them in a little each day, but stay flexible, or devote a specific time to them each week, such as Wednesday afternoons or whenever. Keep a sense of proportion. Do them when you are feeling least effective or most tired.

Diaries and organizers

Good time management takes place in the mind, not in a diary. Nevertheless, a good diary or organizer is probably the most useful tool you can employ to help you to manage yourself well.

There are so many diaries, organizers and software programs available today that the choice can be confusing. While your choice must suit you and the type of work you do, a number of things are vital. In order of priority:

A1 Daily or weekly To Do lists and schedules.

A2 A large space each day for notes.

A3 Somewhere for names, addresses and telephone numbers.

A4 Deciding if you need a portable or desk system.

B Using only one system. This is not always possible but the less time spent copying from one system to another, the better.

B Recording your long-term goals and their tasks, with deadlines.

Most of these requirements can be met by most of the systems now on offer. These include:

- A simple diary from a High Street shop plus a good notebook.

- A paper-based organizer from a time management company. Some major stores now offer their own versions.

- A pocket-sized electronic organizer plus a good notebook.

- A fully networked desktop or laptop computer.

The essential question is: What do you need? Not, what is on offer?

Your notes

Get into the habit of writing most of your notes either in one notebook or on the note pages of your organizer. Include all notes except those recorded in subject or customer files. Record notes of telephone calls, messages, prices, comments, promises, etc. Anything you would have once jotted down on a piece of scrap paper, which would have been lost, should go onto these note pages. This way, notes will never get lost and will always be available to you if you need them in the future. The note pages can be electronic but many people still prefer paper, often a hardcover notebook or 'Day Book' if your diary does not provide suitable pages.

Key Habit: Write all notes in a notebook or in your diary. Never again use scraps of paper for notes.

Tips

- Turn your notes into an invaluable reference document.

- Once a month make a brief index of the important notes and keep these indexes for future reference.

- Cross reference items to other pages by using the dates, eg 'See 7 March'. Use this cross-reference system in your schedule and To Do lists as well.

- Expand your cross-reference system to your e-mail and other systems, eg 'See EM 7 March'.

Example

(Notes page for 7 January)
Nigel telephoned. Meeting on 4 Feb – his office – French contract. 10.00–11.30 am. Bring copy of contract and Ferguson contract for comparison.

(E-mail for 8 January)
Nigel sends a message asking you to bring the Chambers contract to the meeting on 4 Feb as well as the Ferguson contract.

(Schedule for 4 February)
10.00–11.30 am. Meet Nigel. See note 7 Jan. See EM 8 Jan.

Paper, electronic or computer

What type of organizer should you use: paper, electronic or computer? The choice has to be yours unless your company imposes a standard system. None will suit everyone as they all have advantages and disadvantages.

Paper-based organizers

Advantages:

- easy to use;
- can draw sketches, diagrams, maps, as well as write text on the notes page;
- can punch memos, letters, maps, directions, appointment cards, etc and put into the ring system at the right date;
- month or week at-a-glance pages;
- difficult for others to book appointments without your agreement;
- always available, no power requirements.

Disadvantages:

- may need A5 version if a serious user;
- can become bulky and take up a lot of space in a briefcase;
- annual refills are fairly expensive;
- difficult to share information about appointments with others, such as colleagues or a secretary.

Electronic organizers

Advantages:

- portable, take up little room in a briefcase or bag;
- calendar usually extends many years;
- no annual refill costs;

- can exchange information with a personal computer;
- anniversaries and regular appointments can be scheduled automatically weekly, monthly or annually.

Disadvantages:

- slight danger of losing all information through battery failure if user is too casual;
- typing is awkward; may prefer to write notes in a notebook;
- difficult to read in some lighting conditions;
- cannot punch papers and include into organizer;
- difficult or impossible to input sketches, diagrams, mindmaps, etc.

Computer organizers
Advantages:

- easy to exchange appointments with others via your network;
- can check others' schedules when trying to arrange meetings;
- can exchange information with an electronic organizer;
- vast memory available;
- calendar extends many years;
- no annual refill costs;
- fully integrated with other office software such as e-mail and word processing.

Disadvantages:

- not portable if on a desktop machine, bulky if on a laptop;

- others can check your schedule when they want to arrange a meeting. Makes it easier for others to gain access to your time;
- may prefer a paper notebook for the notes page;
- likely to have to buy updated versions every few years;
- likely to use a separate diary because you will not always have the computer with you.

Choose the system that suits you. Try it for at least a month before possibly trying something else but do not keep hopping from one to another. Find one that works for you and stick with it.

5

INTERRUPTIONS

Interruptions are part of working life but they can play havoc with your work unless you learn to control them. Rosemary Stewart, a researcher, found that typical managers were interrupted up to 60 times a day (an average of once every eight minutes) and some suffered much more than that. Most of those interruptions could have waited an hour.

Personal interruptions

Interacting with other people is an essential part of any work, both from a company communications viewpoint and from a social viewpoint. If no one needs to communicate with you, you will not have a job. However, if you spend too much time communicating, especially socializing, you will fail in your job and lose it. Somehow you need to tread a middle path which leaves you in control. This suggests controlling two things: 1) When interruptions are acceptable; and 2) How long they last.

> *Key Habit:* Control interruptions, especially unwanted ones.

Acceptable times

Personal interruptions occur when someone approaches you, pops his or her head round the door and asks something like 'Have you got a minute?' That usually translates into 'Have you got half an hour?'

Being available and accessible to others is essential, but not all the time. Many people pride themselves on having an 'open door'. That is a sensible and noble way of managing except that sometimes, and for lengthy periods, the door must be closed so that you can make progress on your A1 task in your prime time. Being permanently available to others so that they can interrupt you whenever they feel like it is to totally surrender the management of your time. If you have an office with a door, remember that the door has hinges. Use them.

Can you imagine a doctor or a dentist who could be interrupted at any time for something other than an emergency? Somehow you need to be able to signal to others that, at the moment, you are not available so please do not disturb. This is your prime time. How you make that signal will depend on the job and support you have. Not everyone has a secretary to repel boarders, nor even a door they can close.

Possible 'do not disturb' signals:

- a secretary to block access to you and to take messages;
- 'surgery' hours;
- a closed door;

- a 'Do Not Disturb' or 'Prime Time' sign on your door or desk;
- a hat, such as a red cap, or ear muffs to signal 'do not disturb'.

Some companies have official 'Do Not Disturb' signals, especially in open plan offices. One that has been copied more than once is to use red baseball caps. They can be worn for up to two hours at a time to signal prime time.

Of course, to be effective, signals must be understood. You will need to tell others what you are doing and why, and encourage them to do the same.

Tip

If you do not have a secretary, ask nearby colleagues to take messages for you during your prime time. Do the same for them.

Do not try to eliminate interruptions; control them. The secret to control is determination. Remember what you are really there to achieve. Treat your time as the precious resource it is, while being generous in giving it to others when appropriate.

Have you got a minute?

Of course you will still be interrupted, but not as often as previously. When someone does ask 'Have you got a minute?' and you are pressed for time, what can you do?

One widely recommended solution, that works, is to say something like this: 'I'm very pressed for time just now because I'm doing ... which has a deadline of ... If it's really important that we talk now I can spare you five minutes. After that, if it needs longer we can decide on a time to continue'.

The advantages of this technique are:

- it accepts that the interruption is important to the person making it;
- it sets their expectations by telling them about your important task and deadline;
- it sets a time limit;
- a lot can be achieved in five minutes if you get on with it;
- once you know more you can decide whether to extend the time limit now or later; maybe this is your new A1, maybe not;
- it is honest and direct and much better than any amount of so-called 'clever' techniques to put people off.

Ending interruptions

We have all had times when we have wished that a visitor would interrupt us and provide some light relief. Equally we have had times when we wanted people to leave and let us get on with our work. How can you politely persuade someone to leave? How do you end a meeting, tactfully?

You may have come across several 'techniques' but the simplest and most useful is the old-fashioned honest and direct approach: 'Tom, I am sorry but I'm going to have to end our chat. I have a lot on and several deadlines to meet. We've covered everything anyway but if you really think more time is necessary perhaps we can fix another time.'

If you agree that more time is needed schedule it into your diary, otherwise get on with your next task.

Tips

- Set your visitor's expectations at the start by saying you only have a few minutes.
- Sit on the edge of your desk or stand beside it.
- Glance at the clock or your watch.
- Suggest you continue at another time.
- If desperate, gather your papers and leave. Come back in a few minutes in the hope that they have gone.

Prevention

If you know that certain people are a problem:

- Find out why they do it. Solve the root problem and the unnecessary interruptions will stop.
- Log their visits and accumulate the facts: dates, times and reasons. Later sit down with them, explain why their interruptions are sometimes a problem and discuss how to solve that problem.

- Meet at their workplace instead. You gain control because you leave, not them.

Hide

As a last resort pick up your work and go and hide in a conference room or meeting room. However, always be sure that a trusted colleague does know where you are as you may genuinely be wanted in an emergency. If you need access to a computer then try your company's computer training room if there is one. If the company culture will accept it, work at home for one day a week and make that your prime time.

Interrupting others

It is a remarkable fact that while people complain of being interrupted, they cheerfully interrupt others without asking if it is convenient:

- ask if they can spare a few minutes;
- tell them why and how long you think you need;
- together decide whether to do it now or later.

Telephone interruptions

The same principles that apply to personal interruptions also apply to telephone interruptions: control when they are acceptable and how long they last.

When

You cannot know when the telephone will ring, yet you must protect your prime time. The most obvious way to do that is to divert your calls to a colleague during your prime time. Take their calls in return. Assure all callers that their messages will be passed on. Allow your colleagues to use their judgement as to whether a call is important enough to interrupt you.

It is usually better to use a colleague than an answer machine. Treat the machine as a last resort and you will lose fewer callers.

Tip

Secretaries also need prime time. Insist that your secretary has prime time and that his or her telephone calls are diverted either to you or to someone else.

Ending incoming calls

Sometimes it can be a problem ending incoming calls that are either unwanted or have served their purpose. How do you end an incoming call without offending the caller? Callers need to feel confident that their calls have been understood and that action will be taken:

- Take responsibility for the call and ensure that the caller knows you have done so.
- Establish what the caller needs and make notes (in your notebook or diary).

43

- Tell the caller that you are writing it down. That will give them confidence that you are listening.
- End the call by summarizing their message. Tell them what you intend to do and when.
- Thank them for their call.

Inconvenient time

If a call comes at an inconvenient time:

- Apologize to the caller and tell them that it is a bad time and why.
- Offer to call them back and suggest an approximate time: 'Sorry, I have a visitor just now. Can I call you back around 3 o'clock?' An approximate time gives you some freedom. You are not late if you call at five past three.
- Make certain that you do call them even if it is only to say that you have not made any progress as yet. Failure to return a call as promised damages the reputation of your company, and it is far easier to destroy a reputation than to build one.

6

GETTING ORGANIZED

Some people seem to be organized quite naturally while others struggle and work in a permanent mess. There can be many reasons why we lose our organization and control.

Office or work area

Your office or work area can influence your effectiveness. An open plan office encourages communications and interruptions, whereas a closed office can do the opposite.

Furniture

Does your desk or workbench face the corridor? If passers-by make casual or unintended eye contact with you then you will be interrupted more than if they do not. Somehow it seems rude to ignore someone once eye contact has been made. If this is a problem, turn your desk away from the corridor or arrange a partition or screen.

You can walk miles during the course of a day at work. Arrange furniture and equipment so that frequently used routes are short and straight. Make access easiest to the furniture and equipment you use most.

A middle manager complained that he could not complete his work because of the innumerable interruptions he received. After advice he moved his desk so that he faced away from the corridor, placed a poster over the clear glass in his office door and closed his door when he needed prime time. His interruptions reduced and his achievements increased.

Untidy desks

Untidy desks provide distractions that make us interrupt ourselves as well as forcing us to hunt for papers we have mislaid. Anything lying on your work area, desk or bench, which is not connected to the work you are concentrating on, can distract you from your A1.

You have good peripheral vision. That fact alone makes it easy for you to get distracted. You may be working hard at some project only for an unrelated piece of paper or object to catch your eye. Within seconds you have picked it up and can be on the telephone to someone about it. What happened to that A1?

The only papers on your desk should be those needed for the project you are working on. Remove anything else that can distract you, putting papers in filing cabinets and other items in drawers or cupboards. If you are not the perfect housekeeper then at least put unwanted items behind you and out of sight. Nothing will then steal into your peripheral vision and disturb your concentration. It is hard enough as it is to concentrate without adding to the things that can intrude.

> *Key Habit:* Clear your desk of papers unrelated to your immediate work. Either file them or hide them.

Filing system

Does your personal filing system help or hinder your effect-iveness? Could it be organized better? Things you need often should be the easiest and quickest to get hold of. Items that are rarely needed can be placed further away.

Apply the ABC principle to your personal filing system:

- A-items – instant access. Current work that is needed frequently. File in desk drawers or small cabinets that you can reach from your chair.

- B-items – quick access. The majority of your personal files. Readily available in a nearby filing cabinet.

- C-items – slow access. Rarely needed but must be kept. Held further away, even in a storeroom.

What do I do with this?

Most people amass a collection of papers that are not important and not urgent, but they are reluctant to throw them away. You do not know what to do with them so they clutter the in-tray or desktop, even the floor, preventing you from spotting new papers when they arrive.

47

Put all these C-papers into one place, such as a drawer or box, and temporarily forget about them. Check them quickly once a week. Deal with the few that now need action. Throw away as many as you dare. Put the rest back until next week. They are neither lost nor in the way and they will not turn into crises in a week. Put all the 'don't know what to do with it' papers in one place out of sight. Check them weekly.

In a company whose work was classified as 'secret' one manager had a grossly untidy desk. All classified papers were locked into cabinets when the office was unoccupied; otherwise they joined the merry-go-round on top of his desk. One day he and his colleagues missed their lunch break because one secret paper was missing. After hunting for an hour he found it in the midst of his desktop mayhem.

Communications

Poor communications within a company should get the gold watch award for time wasting. This award should apply to all types of communication at all levels.

Tips

- Give clear and unambiguous instructions. Ask recipients to repeat them to you in their own words. If they can do that, they have understood you clearly.

- Concentrate when you are listening. Test the meaning for sense and completeness. Paraphrase important parts to test that you understand correctly.

- Increase the clarity of your written work by using short paragraphs, short sentences and plain language. Ask a colleague to check that the meaning is clear.

Meetings

Make sure that meetings are chaired well or they will waste time and degenerate into talking shops.

Tips

- Invite contributions to the agenda and circulate it in advance. Refuse extra items on the day.
- Set an end time and stick to it.
- Hold short meetings standing up.
- For informal meetings write Action Minutes as you go along. Get agreement as you type them into a computer and print copies at the end.
- Question if you need Any Other Business.
- Remind everyone of the cost of the meeting: roughly £10 per hour for every £10,000 of gross salary represented in the room.

Delegation

Delegation is not the panacea for time management problems that it is sometimes claimed to be but, when treated properly, it is an excellent way to free up some of your time and develop your staff. They, however, must have the time to do the delegated tasks and that may mean educating them to eliminate some of their C-tasks. Use your staff to the full but do not overload them – everyone is pushed for time. Coach them so that they can take on more interesting tasks.

Tips

- Explain what needs to be done and why.
- Set a deadline and mean it.
- Do not tell them how to do the task but allow them to work it out.
- Agree their level of authority and responsibility.
- Let them do it without constant interference.
- Review progress regularly and prevent disasters.
- Coach them gently when necessary.
- Praise them for good work.

Be wary of receiving tasks delegated up to you. Watch out for phrases such as 'Boss, we have a problem.' Too often these generate the answer, 'Leave it with me, I'll sort something out.' Now whose problem is it?

Instead, ask about the problem, listen and then ask for solutions. Discuss these but leave the problem where it belongs – with your staff. Ultimately this saves time for you to do your tasks instead of theirs and it develops their skills as well. Of course there will be occasions when you must take over, but they should be rare.

Other time robbers

- *Computer hassle:* many so-called computer problems result from the operator's lack of skill. Learn to use your software packages well and you will save yourself and others hours of time.

- *Gossiping:* as your attitude towards the importance of your time develops you will increasingly recognize when you are wasting time. If gossiping is your A1 then enjoy it; it will not last long once you remember your real A1.

- *Travelling:* always arrange the optimum route. A mobile telephone is a great time saver but pull off the road to use it. It is more effective to arrive in one piece than to kill yourself by trying to do two things at once when one of them is driving. If you use the train it can be more economical to work in a first-class seat than to stand idle in a second-class coach.

- *Perfectionism:* not everything has to be perfect.

- *Procrastination:* learn to recognize it in yourself; it retreats out of embarrassment.

A busy secretary grew tired of middle-ranking staff asking her to send faxes simply because the fax machine was new and was next to her desk. She wrote a single sheet 'Noddy's Guide to Sending a Fax', gave them all a copy and taped a copy to the fax machine. They got the message and learned to send their own faxes.

During college holidays a private businessman uses college students as chauffeurs. He gets work done while travelling, they are allowed to borrow the car while he is in meetings.

Saying 'no'

So often people are asked to do things by their manager or senior managers and the right and proper answer, in terms of assessed priorities, is 'Sorry, no.' Few people feel they can say that to senior staff and get away with it, so what should they say instead?

One way that you can almost say 'no' and yet retain your reputation as a helpful and concerned employee is to say something such as 'I could do that, but there are consequences that you may not be aware of. For example, I would not then be able to complete... by the promised time and the customer has been assured that it will be ready by then. Also the report you requested yesterday will be late. One of these will have to give. Which do you think it should be?'

This puts the onus on them to decide and take the consequences. All very well, you may be thinking, but my boss will simply say, 'Sorry, but you will have to do them all.'

The answer to this type of common blackmail is simple. If you truly believe what you are saying, that it cannot all be done to the quality required in the time available, then: 1) Give a detailed explanation showing that you are more than willing to do what you can, but the impossible is still impossible. Offer alternative solutions such as getting so and so to help. 2) Use the Cost–Quality–Time triangle. When one is changed at least one of the others is affected. If they cut your time then either the cost goes up because you get some help, or the quality will be reduced.

It is easier to say 'no' to colleagues and subordinates than to senior managers. Apply the basic question of time management to all requests: where does this lie on the scale of priorities? Suggest alternatives if you can but stick to your aim to become more effective by doing the more important things at the expense of the less important ones.

Conclusion

Time – the eternal problem? Yes, but it can be mastered. Use the methods described in this book to regain control of your time, especially at work. Become more effective at doing the things that matter. Recognize that you cannot do everything and let go of most of those Cs. Know what is important, prioritize and make To Do lists work for you. Create prime time and begin with your A1.

Build the habits over the next month and then use the quiz in Chapter 1 to check your progress. Make it a goal to beat the average improvement of 15 points, and do it.

7

SUMMARY

The habits

1 Know what is important to you and what is not. Know the things you want to do – your goals – and plan how and when to do them.

2 Prioritize into three levels: A, B and C; or must, should and could do.

3 Use a written and prioritized daily or weekly To Do list to drive what you do.

4 Your top task is the A1. You decided that. Do it first.

5 Schedule prime time in your diary as a meeting with your A1.

6 Write notes in your diary or in a notebook, not on scraps of paper. Index them monthly.

7 Control interruptions, especially unwanted ones.

8 Clear your desk of papers unrelated to your immediate work.

Additional tips

1   Check how much family, health and recreational time you get in a week.

2   Check your important personal goals every two months and update them.

3   Keep a pocket notebook with you for times when you do not have your proper notebook or diary. Hole punch your notes and put them in your diary.

4   Use sticky notes for messages for other people so that they can stick them into their diaries.

5   Move one of your important tasks forward every day.

6   Remember that it is not that you do not have time, just that you have more important things to do.

7   Don't waste too much precious time watching unimportant programmes on the television. Use TV sensibly for both information and recreation.

8   Use time you spend waiting – either run through a problem in your head or relax and enjoy the view.

9   Ask yourself 'Do I really need to do this?' If not, do something more important.

10 Focus on one task at a time and make a big impression on it.

11 Take a professional approach to difficult or unpleasant tasks. Will avoiding them make them better?

12 Prioritize your files and throw away whatever you can. Assume that 20 per cent of the contents will give you 80 per cent of what you need.

13 Write replies to internal memos on the original and keep a photocopy.

14 Keep asking yourself 'What am I actually trying to achieve?'

15 Be wary of overdoing jobs because of pride. Do they need to be done so well – and take so long?

16 Get colleagues to join you in your concern for effective use of time – theirs and yours. Encourage each other to take time management seriously.

17 Group outgoing telephone calls and turn them into a business task.

18 Assume that something unexpected happens every day.

19 If invited to a meeting, ask yourself if you really need to go.

20 Fix end times as well as start times.

21 Both you and your boss write down your key areas of work without comparing, then sort out differences. Do the same with your subordinates.

22 When staff ask you to solve their problems, ask them to come up with three ideas and one recommendation – in writing.

23 Use the 80:20 rule.

24 Remember other people's important tasks may need a contribution from you, even though they are not your As. Co-operate.

25 Meet occasional visitors in the reception area rather than in your office.